A SIMPLE EXPLANATION OF CONFESSION

CONCORDIA PUBLISHING HOUSE • SAINT LOUIS

Copyright © 2022 Concordia Publishing House
3558 S. Jefferson Ave.
St. Louis, MO 63118-3968

1-800-325-3040 • cph.org

Written by Wayne Palmer

Manufactured in the United States of America

1 2 3 4 5 6 7 8 9 10 31 30 29 28 27 26 25 24 23 22

WHAT IS CONFESSION?

Think back to your childhood. Can you recall a time you did something that made your parents, grandparents, or another adult angry—breaking a vase, trampling a flowerbed, or batting a baseball through a window? Can you recall your thoughts, feelings, and fears?

We all did such things when we were children, and we felt bad or even frightened about them. As we got older, we realized that mom or dad was less angry if we confessed what we did and said it was an accident or a thoughtless behavior. We learned that our best reaction was to simply admit what we had done. We learned to say, "I did it, and I'm sorry."

At the time though, as children, we may have hoped no one would find out, so we avoided saying anything to anyone. Or we may have slid responsibility to someone else, maybe a brother or sister—"Bobby told me to" or "Jenny made me so mad that I broke the vase." Perhaps, to escape punishment, we put on our best innocent face and even claimed, "I didn't do it, and I don't know who did."

Adam

Interestingly, the first human tried this after doing something God had forbidden. Adam acted like a little boy when God came to him.

> *God: "Have you eaten of the tree of which I commanded you not to eat?"*
>
> *Adam: "The woman whom You gave to be with me, she gave me fruit of the tree, and I ate." (Genesis 3:11–12)*

Not much of a confession. Adam tried to shift the blame to his wife, Eve, then even to God Himself for giving Eve to him. That tactic may work with the people around us, but God isn't like our parents, teachers, or family. He knows our thoughts and desires, and He sees everything we do.

Think of criminals who commit crimes but are not caught, or, if they are prosecuted, are not found guilty. Or the person on the murder spree who commits suicide when the police are near. This person thinks he has escaped justice—but he is fooling himself; there is a Judge who immediately rules on his life. This Judge does not require the testimony of witnesses or forensic experts; the ever-present, all-knowing Son of God is a witness to everything we say and do.

> *Can a man hide himself in secret places so that I cannot see him? Declares the Lord. Do I not fill heaven and earth? declares the Lord. (Jeremiah 23:24)*

And more than that, He even knows our inmost thoughts.

> *You know when I sit down and when I rise up; You discern my thoughts from afar. (Psalm 139:2)*

Jesus Christ is the Judge before whom each of us stands when we die. If we do not go before Him in confession in this lifetime, we will face His punishment through all eternity—the never-ending fires of hell.

The idea of confessing our sins to God can be terrifying. It seems like we are just asking to be punished, so we make excuses or try to shift the blame and responsibility a little bit. But lying to God is just another sin that He sees right through—and it adds to our guilt.

What does God want us to do when we mess up and sin against Him and sin against others? Well, He does not want us to try to make up for it by doing good things or by punishing ourselves. King David wrote,

> *The sacrifices of God are a broken spirit; a broken and contrite heart, O God, You will not despise. (Psalm 51:17)*

And the apostle John wrote this promise:

> *If we confess our sins, [God] is faithful and*

just to forgive us our sins and to cleanse us from all unrighteousness. (1 John 1:9)

God doesn't require us to do anything to receive His forgiveness except open up and tell the truth with an open heart—not make excuses, not shift the blame, just tell the truth and admit everything. He is our loving Father who wants to forgive our sins so much that He sent His Son, Jesus, to us. Jesus, God the Son, left the perfection of heaven and lived amid the chaos of humanity on earth. He took our sins, our guilt, and the punishment we deserve upon Himself and suffered and died on the cross. For Jesus' sake, God is more than happy to take away our sins and guilt, to comfort us with His love and forgiveness, and to promise us eternal life with Him.

What Sins Should I Confess?

It is easy to think that God forgives only the specific sins we confess to Him. But that would leave countless sins unforgiven because it is impossible to remember, confess, or even recognize all our sins. The Bible teaches there are even sins we have committed that are hidden from us, sins only God knows.

Who can discern his errors? Declare me innocent from hidden faults. (Psalm 19:12)

Notice, the psalmist could not name his hidden faults, but he asked God to forgive them. Our prayer needs only to be, "Heavenly Father, forgive me all my sins in Jesus' name. Amen."

Then, if particular sins weigh heavily on our hearts, minds, and consciences, we can mention them by name and ask God's forgiveness. And God truly forgives us for Jesus' sake!

We don't need to be in church to confess our sins and ask for God's forgiveness. We can do this privately at any time. But God wants us to be sure and confident of His forgiveness, so He has taught us in the Bible of His full forgiveness. And He established His Church so we can hear and know His forgiveness.

What Is Public Confession?

In traditional Lutheran worship, each Divine Service begins with public confession. None of us is worthy to come into God's presence and receive His blessings. Even if we tried to clean up our lives first, we could never do enough. God invites us to come as we are and bring our failings to Him. And the first thing God does when we come before Him in worship is deal with our sins.

The service begins by calling on the name of our triune (three-in-one) God, who has called each believer by name in Holy Baptism:

> *In the name of the Father, and of the Son, and of the Holy Spirit. Amen.*

Then we hear and say God's promises:

> *If we say we have no sin, we deceive ourselves, and the truth is not in us. But if we confess our sins, God, who is faithful and just, will forgive our sins and cleanse us from all unrighteousness.* (LSB, *p. 151; 1 John 1:8–9)*

Reassured from God's Word that He will forgive us for Jesus' sake, we open our hearts, lay our souls bare before God, and make a public confession. We join our voices with other sinners in words such as these:

> *Most merciful God, we confess that we are by nature sinful and unclean. We have sinned against You in thought, word, and deed, by what we have done and by what we have left undone. We have not loved You with our whole heart; we have not loved our neighbors as ourselves. We justly deserve Your present and eternal punishment. For the sake of Your Son, Jesus Christ, have mercy on us. Forgive us, renew us, and lead us, so that we may delight in Your will and walk in Your ways to the glory of Your holy name. Amen.* (LSB, *Divine Service, Setting 1)*

Notice that we make no excuses. We admit to God that we alone are responsible for our sins and that they come from our sinful nature. We also admit our failure to do the good things God requires. This confession does not mention specific sins—but while we are praying, we can think of particular sins that weigh heavily on our hearts.

Also, notice what we don't do in confession. We don't make resolutions, pledges, or promises to God. We don't say, "If You will forgive my sins, I promise never to repeat them." We can't keep such promises because of our sinful nature. But God doesn't look for promises; He looks for true confession, our open and broken hearts. Then God takes away our sin and guilt. That is often called absolution. To absolve means "to declare a person free of all blame, guilt, and responsibility." In the Divine Service, the pastor speaks God's forgiveness in either of two ways—to the whole congregation together:

In the mercy of almighty God, Jesus Christ was given to die for us, and for His sake God forgives us all our sins. To those who believe in Jesus Christ He gives the power to become the children of God and bestows on them the Holy Spirit. May the Lord, who has begun this good work in us, bring it to completion in the day of our Lord Jesus Christ.

or to each believer individually:

Almighty God in His mercy has given His Son to die for you and for His sake forgives you all your sins. As a called and ordained servant of Christ, and by His authority, I therefore forgive you all your sins in the name of the Father and of the Son and of the Holy Spirit. Amen. (LSB, *p. 151)*

Where Does God's Forgiveness Come From?

God does not forgive us because of what we do to try to make up for our sins. He forgives us only because of what His Son, Jesus Christ, has already done for us. Jesus carried all the sins of all time to the cross and suffered their punishment there.

But when Christ had offered for all time *a single sacrifice for sins, He sat down at the right hand of God. (Hebrews 10:12, emphasis added)*

This includes all future sins until the end of time. Historically, our Lutheran Divine Service is designed with multiple times when we can confess our sins and hear of God's full and complete forgiveness for Jesus' sake, including

- the Invocation, with its sign of the cross that reminds us of our Baptism, where God washed away our sins in the blood of His Son, Jesus, adopted us as His own children, and filled us with His Holy Spirit;
- Confession and Absolution, when we confess all our sins and hear the pastor assure us that God has forgiven our sins for Jesus' sake;
- Scripture readings that remind us of other sinners who received forgiveness from God;
- hymns;
- congregational prayers;
- the sermon; and
- physically, in Jesus' true body and blood in Holy Communion.

How wonderful it is, week after week, to hear the assurance that God has forgiven all our sins through His Son, Jesus Christ. But what if you're carrying in your heart a huge sin and the terrible fallout from it? What if you did something that drove away your best friend, destroyed your family, wrecked your marriage, alienated your children, or carelessly caused someone's death? What if you are filled with fear and dread of Christ's return and the Confession and Absolution in the service are not quieting your fears?

When Should I Seek Private Confession?

We are not required to ever meet privately with the pastor to confess and receive forgiveness for our sins. In fact, if the forgiveness you receive in worship is enough to leave you free of guilt or fear of punishment, then you do not need private confession.

But if you are troubled by a particular sin, Jesus established private confession with His pastors so we can hear that He forgives the sins that are weighing heaviest on us.

Come now, let us reason together, says the Lord*: though your sins are like scarlet, they shall be as white as snow; though they are red like crimson, they shall become like wool. (Isaiah 1:18)*

Why such dark, staining red? Because God wants us to think of the vilest sins we can imagine—bloodshed and murder. He wants us to think of the kinds of sins that can easily drive a sinner to despair and doubt that God could ever forgive us. Yet, in Christ Jesus, all that bloodguilt is washed away, and we are left spotless and clean.

What Qualifies the Pastor to Forgive My Sins?

The evening after Jesus rose from the dead, He appeared to His disciples, who were gathered behind locked doors. After greeting them, He spoke these words:

Receive the Holy Spirit. If you forgive the sins of any, they are forgiven them; if you withhold forgiveness from any, it is withheld. (John 20:22–23)

Martin Luther called this the Office of the Keys, building on Jesus' words to Peter and His disciples in Matthew 16:19:

> *I will give you the keys of the kingdom of heaven, and whatever you bind on earth shall be bound in heaven, and whatever you loose on earth shall be loosed in heaven.*

This authority is given to the Church, which entrusts it to her ordained pastors, who speak by Christ's command and in His place.

But what gives the pastor the right to forgive my sins? Isn't that between me and God alone?

It certainly would not be any of the pastor's business if Christ had not given this command. And it isn't the pastor's business, or Christ's intent, for us to go through a catalog of all our sins, dredging them up to confess to the pastor.

Jesus' purpose in private confession is to reassure us when we are troubled over specific things we have said and done. We've all said devastating things that have shattered relationships or performed careless deeds that harmed others. Where can we find comfort and rest for these? Through the gift of private confession.

But how can the pastor assure me my sins are forgiven?

Jesus didn't carry just some sins to the cross; He carried all of them.

Some Christian denominations argue that Jesus couldn't have borne the punishment for all sins, otherwise God would be unjust to punish Jesus, then turn around and punish unbelievers in hell for those very same sins.

That makes logical sense to our limited minds, but it isn't in the Bible. Instead, God's Word says, "He died for all" (2 Corinthians 5:15), and "He is the propitiation for our sins, and not for ours only but also for the sins of the whole world" (1 John 2:2).

And because Jesus carried all the sins of all people of all time and paid completely for each and every one of them, there is forgiveness for each sin we have committed—no matter how devastating or grievous it was.

But what if my sin is so shocking the pastor will send me away in anger and shame?

That, my friend, is not going to happen. How can you be sure? Because the pastor is a sinner too. And he knows that in God's eyes the smallest sin is no different than the largest. After all, Adam and Eve plucked fruit from a tree God had forbidden them to touch. That may seem pretty small to us, but it was an open act of rebellion against God's Word and promise. They listened to Satan's temptation and took Satan's word over God's Word. Sadly, it resulted in all the pain, suffering, decay, and death in the world today.

Any act of sin, however great or small in our estimation, is an act of rebellion against the God of the universe. When we sin, we bring God's judgment for our rebellion down on ourselves and are without excuse. The pastor will remind you of the good news that God chose to punish His Son instead of you and me.

The pastor also pledges to keep our confessions confidential, promising not to divulge them to anyone else. This gives us confidence to confess our sins.

The other thing pastors can do in private confession is remind us that some of the most wonderful people in the Bible committed some of the most horrendous sins—and God still forgave them. Your pastor may remind you of these people to assure you that since God forgave them for Jesus' sake, He certainly can forgive you for Jesus' sake.

King David

Consider King David. When he was still young, too young to serve in Israel's army, he trusted God and courageously rescued Israel by killing the giant Goliath with a stone and a sling. Later, he was a good and faithful king over Israel. God even said about him,

> *I have found in David the son of Jesse a man after My heart, who will do all My will. (Acts 13:22)*

But King David had a dark side too. One spring morning when his army was off at war, he surveyed his capital city of Jerusalem from the palace roof.

That's when he spied a beautiful woman bathing on her roof. As a married man, he should have turned and walked away, but instead, he sent messengers to ask who she was.

When he learned she was Bathsheba, the wife of Uriah, a faithful officer in his army, he still had time to stop and turn away. But he let his lust have the upper hand, had her brought to him, and he slept with her. A married man having an affair with a married woman was two sins. He then sent her back to her house, thinking no one would ever know of his adultery and that would be the end of it.

But right about the time he thought it was all over, she sent him word that she was pregnant. Of course, David was troubled by the news. He quickly summoned her husband, Uriah, to return to Jerusalem. This was the perfect time to confess what he had done and ask for Uriah's forgiveness, but David had a plan to cover up his sin.

He asked Uriah for a report on the war effort, then told him to go home and enjoy the night with his wife. He was confident Uriah would sleep with his beautiful wife and think the baby was his. But the next morning, David learned that Uriah hadn't gone home—he had pitched a tent on the palace grounds and slept alone. David asked why he didn't go home, and Uriah told him,

> *The ark and Israel and Judah dwell in booths, and my lord Joab and the servants of my lord are camping in the open field. Shall I then go to my house, to eat and to drink and to lie with my wife? As you live, and as your soul lives, I will not do this thing. (2 Samuel 11:11)*

David's cheeks should have burned with guilt standing before this officer of his who was so loyal and trusting. It should have squeezed the confession out of him. Instead, David doubled down.

> *David invited him, and he ate in his presence and drank, so that he made him drunk. (2 Samuel 11:13)*

It should have worked. Uriah was so drunk that surely he would stagger home, then not remember whether he had slept with Bathsheba. Later, he would naturally assume the baby was his. But no;

even drunk, Uriah did what was right. He went back to his tent and spent the night alone.

God kept spoiling David's plot, pushing him toward repentance. But David took his cover-up deeper—and darker. He wrote a letter to Joab, the commander of his army, and sent it by the hand of Uriah. In the letter, he wrote,

> *Set Uriah in the forefront of the hardest fighting, and then draw back from him, that he may be struck down, and die. (2 Samuel 11:15)*

As if adultery wasn't bad enough, David added murder to his sins. Faithful, trusting Uriah never saw it coming. He handed his death sentence to Joab and died in battle the next day.

When the news got back to David, he gave Bathsheba a brief time to mourn her husband's death, then took her to be his own wife.

Oh, the people of Jerusalem were impressed. "Look at our good king David. He felt so bad about the poor, pregnant widow of Uriah that he took her to be his own wife." David had everything worked out. Everyone was fooled, the whole affair was covered up, everything was fine—except it wasn't.

When God created humans, He wrote His Law on our hearts and gave us a conscience, which fills us with guilt and fear when we break that Law. Our fear and guilt show us that God is holy and perfectly just. In the following months, David couldn't quiet his conscience, as he later wrote in Psalm 32.

> *When I kept silent, my bones wasted away through my groaning all day long. For day and night Your hand was heavy upon me; my strength was dried up as by the heat of summer. (vv. 3–4)*

In mercy, God sent the prophet Nathan to bring the confession to David's lips. David didn't spell out the full extent of his crime. He didn't have to; God already knew it all. Nathan said,

> *Why have you despised the word of the LORD, to do what is evil in His sight? You have struck down Uriah the Hittite with the sword and have taken his wife to be your wife and have killed him with the sword of the Ammonites. (2 Samuel 12:9)*

David was done hiding and making excuses. He answered, "I have sinned against the Lord." David described his response in these words of Psalm 32:

> *I acknowledged my sin to You, and I did not cover my iniquity; I said, "I will confess my transgressions to the Lord," and You forgave the iniquity of my sin. (v. 5)*

Nathan relayed God's forgiveness, or absolution, to David.

> *The Lord also has put away your sin; you shall not die. (2 Samuel 12:13)*

There were heavy consequences David had to pay. The baby died soon after birth. David's children later turned against one another. There was rape and a revenge killing, and one of his sons even rose up in rebellion and seized David's throne for a brief time.

David wrote two psalms about that horrific time in his life, psalms we can use to confess our deepest, darkest sins and be assured of God's full and free forgiveness. We already read part of Psalm 32. The other is Psalm 51:

Have mercy on me, O God,
According to Your steadfast love;
According to Your abundant mercy
Blot out my transgressions.
Wash me thoroughly from my iniquity,
And cleanse me from my sin.

For I know my transgressions;
And my sin is ever before me.
Against You, You only, have I sinned
And done what is evil in Your sight,
So that You may be justified in Your words
And blameless in Your judgment.
Behold, I was brought forth in iniquity,
and in sin did my mother conceive me.
Behold, You delight in truth in the inward being,
And You teach me wisdom in the secret heart.

Purge me with hyssop, and I shall be clean;
Wash me, and I shall be whiter than snow,
Let me hear joy and gladness;
Let the bones that You have broken rejoice.
Hide Your face from my sins,
And blot out all my iniquities.
Create in me a clean heart, O God,
And renew a right spirit within me.
Cast me not away from Your presence,

And take not Your Holy Spirit from me.
Restore to me the joy of Your salvation,
And uphold me with a willing spirit.
(vv. 1–12)

Imagine hearing that God forgave and restored David after those horrendous crimes! God restored him so thoroughly that Jesus delighted to be called the Son of David. If God could forgive David his sin, surely He can forgive you yours!

The Repentant Thief

When Jesus was nailed to the cross, two criminals were hung on either side of Him. At first, both ridiculed Jesus, but then one changed his mind.

One of the criminals who were hanged railed at Him, saying, "Are You not the Christ? Save Yourself and us!" But the other rebuked him, saying, "Do you not fear God, since you are under the same sentence of condemnation? And we indeed justly, for we are receiving the due reward of our deeds; but this man has done nothing wrong." And he said, "Jesus, remember me when You come into Your kingdom." And

He said to him, "Truly, I say to you, today you will be with Me in paradise." (Luke 23:39–43)

The repentant thief had nothing to offer Jesus. He had no time or opportunity to make amends for his crimes and sins. Yet Jesus forgave him and assured him he would be with Jesus in paradise upon his death that very day. If Jesus could forgive the criminal being executed at His side, He can forgive you all your sins.

Peter

Another case with a man who committed a seemingly unforgivable sin was one of Jesus' chosen apostles, Simon Peter. He was the natural leader among the Twelve. Bold and brash, Peter often acted before thinking things through.

The night Jesus was arrested, Peter followed behind the guards to learn what would happen to Him. When he got into the courtyard among the guards, everything started going wrong. Matthew 26 records the scene:

> *Now Peter was sitting outside in the courtyard. And a servant girl came up to him and said, "You also were with Jesus the Galilean." But he denied it before them all, saying, "I do not know what you mean." (vv. 69–70)*

Things were getting too uncomfortable, so Peter nonchalantly tried to slip out the entrance.

> *And when he went out to the entrance, another servant girl saw him, and she said to the bystanders, "This man was with Jesus of Nazareth." And again he denied it with an oath: "I do not know the man." (vv. 71–72)*

Matthew didn't record Peter's oath, but it was probably something like, "I swear to the God of Abraham, Isaac, and Jacob, I do not know Him." An oath was a very serious thing to Jews. They believed that when they took an oath, they were asking God to search their hearts and punish them if they were lying. Of course, Peter wasn't thinking that far ahead. He was desperate to save himself. He could only hope the oath would be enough to quiet the onlookers' suspicions. But it wasn't.

> *After a little while the bystanders came up and said to Peter, "Certainly you too are one of them, for your accent betrays you." (v. 73)*

That was the last straw—Peter was a northerner, a Galilean. And down here among the southerners in Jerusalem, his accent drew a lot of attention. He did the only thing he could think to do:

> *Then he began to invoke a curse on himself and to swear, "I do not know the man." (v. 74)*

Peter's curse would probably be something like "May God strike me down right now if I am lying to you." Peter was still speaking the words when the rooster crowed for a second time with the breaking dawn. Luke tells us,

> *And the Lord turned and looked at Peter. And Peter remembered the saying of the Lord, how He had said to him, "Before the rooster crows today, you will deny Me three*

times." And he went out and wept bitterly. (Luke 22:61–62)

Oh, the shame, guilt, and sorrow that racked Peter! He had sworn to Jesus he would rather die than deny Him. But when the moment of truth came, Peter withered, his courage failed, and he lied to servant girls.

How could Peter ever stand before Jesus again? How could he stand up and declare Jesus' name to the crowds in Jerusalem? He needed the assurance of the Lord's forgiveness, and that is exactly what Jesus gave when He rose from the dead. We read in the great resurrection chapter of Luke 24 a report from the gathered disciples:

"The Lord has risen indeed, and has appeared to Simon!" (Luke 24:34)

On the afternoon of Easter, Jesus made a special appearance to Simon Peter all alone. But their conversation is not recorded in Scripture. We should consider it to be a private confession and absolution between a pastor and a sinner.

And Jesus' forgiveness made all the difference for Peter. It freed him to be a strong leader of the Christian Church when the Holy Spirit came at Pentecost. That is the freedom and the peace you get from confession—to know God loves you, forgives you for Jesus' sake, and promises to be with you and bring you to live with Him through all eternity when Christ returns.

Conclusion

God knows each and every one of us is a sinner. We stir up His anger and deserve nothing but His punishment here on earth and forever in the fires of hell. But God loves us too much to let that happen to us—so He sent His Son, Jesus, to become a human, to live among us, and to take our sin and guilt upon Himself so that on the cross, God could punish Him in our place. Because of Jesus' death and resurrection, you are free from your sin. You never need to fear God's punishment.

Jesus established His Christian Church so that through the Word of God and the Sacraments of Baptism and Holy Communion, He can reassure us of God's forgiveness. Whether that comes through public confession or private confession and absolution, you can know with certainty that God has forgiven your sins, and you can live in peace and joy, serving God and your neighbor in gratitude and love.